The Ministry of The Lector

CAROLINE M. THOMAS

RESOURCE PUBLICATIONS, INC.
San Jose, California

© 2009 Resource Publications, Inc. All rights reserved. No part of this book may be photocopied or otherwise reproduced without permission from the publisher. For reprint permission, contact:

>   Reprint Department
>   Resource Publications, Inc.
>   160 E. Virginia St. #290
>   San Jose, CA 95112-5876
>   (408) 286-8505
>   (408) 287-8748 fax

Library of Congress Cataloging-in-Publication Data

Thomas, Caroline M., 1943-
The ministry of the lector / Caroline M. Thomas.
    p. cm.
Includes bibliographical references (p.   ).
ISBN-13: 978-0-89390-689-4 (pbk.)
ISBN-10: 0-89390-689-1 (pbk.)
1. Lay readers--Catholic Church. I. Title.

BX1915.T56 2009
264'.02--dc22
                                    2009047912

Printed in the United States of America
09 10 11 12 13 | 5 4 3 2 1

Cover illustration: George Collopy
Illustrations: George Collopy and Helen St Paul
Design and production: Kenneth Guentert, The Publishing Pro, LLC
Copyeditor: Kenneth Guentert

Excerpts from the *Lectionary for Mass for Use in the Dioceses of the United States of America, second typical edition* © 2001, 1998, 1997, 1986, 1970 Confraternity of Christian Doctrine, Inc., Washington, DC. Used with permission. All rights reserved. No portion of this text may be reproduced by any means without permission in writing from the copyright owner. (Emphasis has been added to demonstrate reading techniques.)

Contents

Preface	vii
Chapter One: The Importance of the Sunday Assembly	1
Chapter Two: A Variety of Ministerial Roles	4
Chapter Three: Items Lectors Use	8
Chapter Four: The Structure of the Liturgy and the Lector's Role	10
Chapter Five: Preparation	15
Training	15
Study	16
Practice	19
Last-Minute Details	20
After Mass	22
Chapter Six: Specific Techniques	23
Practice Techniques	24
Emphasis	26
Tempo	27
Eye Contact	28
Conviction	32
Energy	32
Inflection	33
Movement	38
Silence	39
Focus	41
After Mass	42

Chapter Seven: Preparing to Lector—A Checklist	44
Lector's Prayer	51
Continued Growth in Ministry	52
Notes	54

Preface

So you have been asked, or have otherwise agreed, to be a lector. Or maybe you have been ministering as a lector for some time already and can use a fresh approach. What does that mean? Where do you start?

This book will help you understand your role within the liturgy and within the assembly of God's people. It will also give you suggestions on how to make your ministry more meaningful, for yourself and for the assembly. The goal is to make God's word come alive with meaning for God's people, to make it alive and transforming for them and for you. Rev. Edward Foley, Capuchin, is a professor of liturgy and music and the founding director of the ecumenical doctor of ministry program at the Catholic Theological Union, Chicago, Illinois. In his recording *The Eucharist as Mystagogy Volume V,* he equates the importance of the Liturgy of the Word with that of the Liturgy of the Eucharist:

> For just as later we will
>   *raise* the elements,
>   *hymn* the elements,
> and *share* the elements in sacramental Communion,
> so in this moment do we *raise* the word,
>   *hymn* the word,
>   and *share* the word as auditory communion
>   with the one Christ who—
>   at least in Johannine cosmology—
>   *was* the Word long before he was rendered in the flesh.[1]

Chapter One

The Importance of the Sunday Assembly

We are called by God to gather together in Christ's name. Every time we gather, we become the Body of Christ, and Christ is present as our head. In celebrating the eucharistic liturgy, what we do makes us what we are. Through ritual we symbolize and actualize ourselves as the Body of Christ, the church.

When we assemble for Mass as God's family, we begin as most family gatherings do. We greet one another, and we begin to tell our stories. This storytelling helps us to reconnect with one another by remembering our common history. We remember other members of our extended families who may no longer be with us and whose memory we cherish. We re-establish ourselves as a family with a common history when we come together for Christmas, Thanksgiving, a graduation, a baptism, or just a family picnic.

The Introductory Rites begin this process. By greeting one another as we come in and by singing together during the opening song, we reconnect ourselves to one another as members of God's family. We transition from being individuals to being part of the Body of Christ, called together by God to worship in Christ's name.

You may think of yourself as separate and distinct from the gathered assembly by virtue of your role as a liturgical minister, but this is not the case. First and foremost, we are all members of this assembly. Ideally, if you are a lector, you should be seated in the assembly and come up to minister at the ambo from that location. Even the presider, the priest, is first of all a member of the assembly. He has a specific role to play as the presider or leader of the assembly's prayer. He exercises this role from the presider's chair, the ambo, or altar. Whenever he is not engaged in this role, he is a member of the general assembly and does what members of the assembly do. For example, he will listen to the readings with everyone else as the lector proclaims them. Some presiders make a point of demonstrating this by turning to face the lector at the ambo.

During the first and second readings, the lector is the leader of the assembly. All are recipients of God's spoken word. That word is spoken to and for the presider as much as to the rest of us. Presumably, the lector (or the priest or deacon in the case of the gospel) has studied it in advance. Still, as it is proclaimed, the word sounds anew. The word is living and can be heard differently each time. There are always new insights and inspirations to be gained. The word is new and fresh, a living word proclaimed by the living lector, and given new life each time.

Your role as lector is a ministry. Ministry is service to God's people. This role is not a cause for pride in your ability or an opportunity to "shine." It is a cause for humility because God, through God's church, has called you to speak in God's name, proclaiming God's truth and story. Do you find you don't feel worthy of the role? You are a bit like the prophets of the Old Testament, who were called to speak in God's name but did not always feel up to the task. Nonetheless, they experienced the urgency of the call. Humility is not to be understood as self-denigration but to be experienced as a posture of honesty before God, acknowledging your gifts in gratitude to the One who has given them.

The assembly is the starting point for ministry. The assembly is the context within which other ministries are defined. Without the assembly, there is no framework for your ministry as lector or for any other liturgical ministry. Your proclamation of the word takes place in the midst of this assembly and is in service to it. Your ministry derives its purpose and goal from the assembly. Without the assembly, there is no need for the ministry of lector.

Chapter Two
A Variety of Ministerial Roles

A number of liturgical ministries are exercised during Mass. The role of the priest is that of **presider**, the one who orchestrates the whole and leads our prayer. The prayers that the priest verbalizes, which we call the "presidential prayers," belong to all of us. He voices them in our name. If we listen, we realize that none of these prayers are spoken in first person singular but always in first person plural. He speaks for all of us. It is important to pray along with the priest. The church has developed these prayers from a universal perspective, which is obvious when we listen. They are not the prayers of an individual but of all of us. The presider leads us in our *spoken* prayer.

The **musicians** lead us in our *sung* prayer. The members of the assembly are the primary music ministers of the liturgy. Those whom we call "music ministers" enable the musical ministry of the entire gathered assembly. If their ministry is about "performance" and in some way limits the participation of the assembly, then their role is a distortion. This does not mean the assembly must sing every song. Sometimes an inspirational or meditative song contributes to the assembly's participation, even though the participation is one of silent listening and reflecting. However, the primary job of the music minister is to lead us in our sung prayer during Mass. Musicians should not usurp the role of the gathered assembly in a showcase of their own talents. From this perspective, the selection of songs is important. The songs are to support the focus of the readings. They put prayers on our lips that augment our understanding of those readings. They are a heart-felt response of praise and gratitude for God's goodness.

The role of the **extraordinary ministers of holy communion** is to facilitate our sharing in the Body and Blood of Christ in physical form under the signs of bread and wine. Practically speaking, their job is to keep the distribution of holy communion from taking too long. In addition, their job is to be welcoming and accepting—and to minister God's love along with Christ's Body and Blood. They do this through their eye contact, tone of voice, and facial expression.

Hospitality ministers (ushers & greeters) also serve to communicate God's care. They do this by making the environment comfortable (adjusting heat or air conditioning, opening or closing windows), neat (straightening up books and picking up debris before and after Mass), and welcoming (greeting worshippers at the door or even in the parking lot, assisting them to find a seat, and providing direction during communion).

Your role as **lector** is to tell our story, to remind us of our spiritual history. You are the community's storyteller. The story reminds us of who we are in relationship to one another and to God. Remembering the history of God's goodness to God's people establishes the foundation from which we proceed to the eucharistic part of the liturgy. The Liturgy of the Word sets up the premise for the Liturgy of the Eucharist. In remembering what God has done for us in the past, we are moved to the gratitude that we express in "doing Eucharist." The word *Eucharist* is from the Greek for "thanksgiving," and this is what we do in that second half of the liturgy: give God our thanks and praise. In fact, in the dialogue at the very beginning of the Eucharistic Prayer, we respond that it is right that we give our thanks and praise.

The entire liturgy is structured as call and response. The presider greets us, "The Lord be with you," and we respond, "And also with you." The responsorial psalm responds to the first reading. Our recitation of the Creed and invocation at the prayer of the faithful are responses to the readings and homily we have heard. The second half of the liturgy, the Liturgy of the Eucharist, is a response to the first half, the Liturgy of the Word. The readings in the Liturgy of the Word must be proclaimed in such a way that they elicit the response of praise and thanksgiving, which is the Liturgy of the Eucharist.

The assembly has a role in the Liturgy of the Word as well. As described in *The Ministry of the Assembly* (Resource Publications, Inc., 2008), the members of the assembly minister to the lector as he or she is proclaiming. Sitting is a posture of receptivity. It connotes an openness to what is being proclaimed, a willingness to accept it. The members of the assembly have a role that goes beyond passive receptivity, however. They are participating in the liturgy at that time by actively listening, which is more than just paying attention. Active listening requires that we express our receptivity by our eye contact, facial expression, and posture. For you to proclaim the word most effectively, you must be well aware that people are actively receiving that proclamation. The act of lectoring requires energy—from you as you proclaim the word and from members of the assembly as they listen intensely. Those who proclaim and those who listen are both converted through the process. It is an interactive event. The lector not only "gives" the reading to the assembly, but the members of the assembly "give back" to the lector through their appreciative attentiveness.

Edward Foley notes that this is not always the fact and writes that

> The impassive faces of both ministry and assembly
>   suggest widespread oblivion to the fact
>   that these auditory missives are, in truth,
>   Spirit-dipped projectiles from the God of Jesus Christ,
>   stretched on the bow of a divine cupid
>   and aimed at the center of our hearts.[2]

Your ministry is intended to eliminate this impassivity and oblivion and to help these divine projectiles find their human mark.

Chapter Three
Items Lectors Use

It is important to know the proper names of the items you will use in your ministry. This facilitates communication. The **ambo** is one of those names. Sometimes it is referred to as the "pulpit" or "lectern," two terms that have connotations different from "ambo." The pulpit seems to imply preaching, and the lectern is a place of teaching, not necessarily in a church setting. However, the ambo is the place where the word of God is proclaimed. Following this definition, it is slightly raised from the floor level to emphasize its importance and to improve its visibility to the assembly.

Accordingly, the ambo is used only for the first reading, responsorial psalm (also God's word), the second reading, the gospel, the homily (breaking open God's word for the community), and the intercessions (our baptismal response to God's word).

The **lectionary** is the book from which the first and second readings are proclaimed. Although all the readings are taken from sacred Scripture, the lectionary is not the Bible. It is a collection of brief excerpts, most of which have been assembled in a deliberate order and specific relationship to one another. (The second reading is not selected to relate to the gospel. Often, it is a sequential reading from Sunday to Sunday through a particular epistle or letter in the New Testament.) The Sunday readings rotate on a three-year cycle and the weekday readings on a two-year cycle.

When preparing for a particular Sunday, consider each reading within the context of the Scripture from which it was taken *and* in relationship to the other readings of that day. This includes the psalm. Take into account the readings of the previous weeks as well as those that will be heard in the week and weeks to come. The lectionary builds its own relationship among the readings, and they need to be proclaimed and heard within this relationship. In addition, think about the community you will be proclaiming to and any events that have affected this community. All of these considerations should be part of your preparation for any given Sunday.

The Book of the Gospels contains the gospels read on Sundays and holy days. There are no other readings in it. The gospels are also contained in the lectionary along with the other readings and the psalms. *The Book of the Gospels* is to be processed in at the beginning of Mass. If there is a deacon, he will carry it in procession because proclamation of the gospel is specific to his ministry. In the absence of a deacon, the lector will process in with it. *The Book of the Gospels* is not processed out at the conclusion of the liturgy because the members of the assembly have welcomed the word of God into their lives and take it out into the world.

Chapter Four
The Structure of the Liturgy and the Lector's Role

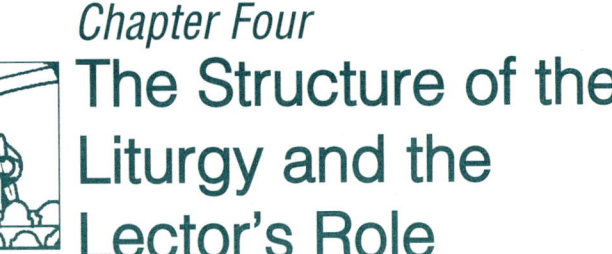

The liturgy begins with the **Introductory Rites**, which start with the gathering. This part of the liturgy is the process by which we form ourselves into the assembled Body of Christ. Ideally, those whose role is to welcome people coming into the church building should greet everyone, especially those they don't know. There will be other opportunities to speak with friends. The greeting given to the stranger may be the one thing that makes him or her feel welcomed and accepted as part of this celebrating community. It is important that all feel welcomed, that all feel comfortable enough in this community to be able to open themselves up to the word and to express themselves in song and voiced prayer. They need to feel comfortable enough to exercise their ministry as members of the assembly.

As a lector, it is your role not only to greet others but also to let yourself be shaped into this assembled Body of Christ. You can do this by greeting people as they come in for Mass and connecting yourself with them. You can also do this by singing the gathering song during the procession of ministers. If you are processing in with *The Book of the Gospels*, you may not be able to sing unless you have memorized the song. If you are processing up with the book, hold it high in a position of prominence, straight up and down with the front cover facing you. This way, the people will be able to see the cover as you process up toward the altar. In addition, when you reach the altar, you can set the book down without flipping it around. If you are not carrying *The Book of the Gospels* but processing in with the other ministers, bow at the foot of the altar with them.

Once you have placed *The Book of the Gospels* on the altar and gone to your pew, you can join the rest of the community in song if you have not yet been able to do. One of the primary purposes of this song is to join everyone together. (We even breathe together when we sing.) This is supposed to include everyone in the procession as well as the assembly. For this reason, the gathering song should continue for a verse or two after the presider arrives at his chair. He is a member of the community, united to all gathered, not separate and somehow "above." His participation in the gathering song connects him to the rest of the assembly and establishes his role as part of the assembly. Because he does not carry anything in the procession, he can carry a songbook and sing while processing.

What happens during this part of the liturgy sets the tone for what follows. The gathering song is far more than a musical accompaniment to the entrance procession. It bonds us to one another, focuses us on the feast or season (especially during the Advent, Christmas, Lent, and Easter seasons), and prepares us mentally and emotionally for the communal worship to follow.

We proceed through the rest of the Introductory Rites: the greeting, the Act of Penitence or the Rite of Blessing and

Sprinkling of Water, the Gloria, if there is one, and the Opening Prayer. Through all of these we participate as members of the assembly, joining fully in song and prayer. In this way we prepare ourselves to listen to God's word.

During the **Liturgy of the Word,** you may be proclaiming the first reading. If you are not, you listen with the rest of the assembly to the reading so you can hear what God has to say to us this day. The word is for everyone, including the lectors and the presider, who also should be listening attentively. Even when you proclaim the word, it still forms you. Sometimes, even in the act of proclamation, you hear something new in it. Edward Foley writes:

> To enter into—and not simply "attend"—the Liturgy of the Word
> > is to experience real communion with the God of Jesus Christ,
> > for this word and the liturgical unit which bears its name
> > are not just "about" God: They are "of" God.
> And to participate in
> > and not merely listen to the Liturgy of the Word
> > is to enter into a unique union with the Holy One;
> > for in this ritual dialogue,
> > God not only speaks *to* us
> > but, like that first act of creation recounted in Genesis,
> > God definitively speaks *us* into being as hearers of the word.
> Thus, to be spiritually attuned
> > (and not just physically *present* for the Liturgy of the Word)
> > is to understand intimately
> > that the table of the word is no pseudo-presence
> > but trustworthy communion with the God whom we do not see
> > but whom we are most privileged to *hear*.[3]

The Structure of the Liturgy and the Lector's Role

You need to be aware of this for yourself as a listener and even more so for yourself as the proclaimer of this living, loving, and transforming word of God.

Then, along with the rest of the assembly, you sing the psalm response, which is chosen to help us understand the readings. It is designed to set the context within which we hear them. This is one reason for considering the psalm when you practice your reading for the week. It will ground your proclamation by helping you understand the context within which this week's readings were chosen.

Now, with others, you greet the gospel with the joyous alleluia or, during Lent, with the alternate gospel acclamation. We honor Christ by standing in anticipation of his presence in the living word of the gospel. We listen attentively to the gospel itself, which you have also read in advance as part of your preparation. You may in fact hear something new as it is proclaimed by another.

We then sit to receive the homily, which will make God's word relevant to our daily lives. We respond with our profession of faith in the Creed, and exercise our baptismal right in praying for the needs of the world in the general intercessions.

If this is your week to lector, you have the privilege of ministering to God's people through your proclamation. You make your faith witness to God's word. The rest of the Liturgy of the Word is directed to us as members of the assembly. We all sit or stand and attentively receive the message that God wants us to hear on this occasion.

The **Liturgy of the Eucharist** follows. We present ourselves with the bread and wine and with our own financial donation to the parish and for the poor. As lector, you do all that the assembly does, pray the prayers, and sing the songs. Even though the presider is voicing the prayers, they are our prayers. They are all in first person plural and said in our name. The action of the priest is the action of the community. We make the prayers our own and participate enthusiastically in the spoken and sung parts that are ours. We receive Christ's Body and Blood and open ourselves to the transformation made possible through this sacrament.

The **Concluding Rites** send us forth into the world to bring Christ, whom we have shared in word and sacrament, to others through our words and actions during the week. If we have been open to Christ's presence during the liturgy and have taken to heart what we have heard and experienced, it should transform us and shape who we are in our relationships and personal interactions.

Lectors participate in the entire liturgy as members of the assembly, called by God to be ever more intimately united with Christ and with one another. It is as a member of this assembly that you are called forth by this community to minister to them for their benefit through your proclamation. It is not something that you "choose" to do. It is something you are called to by virtue of God's gifts to you. God's gifts are always given for the benefit of the community. The community calls you forth to exercise them.

Chapter Five
Preparation

Serious preparation is necessary to fulfill your ministry well. The three primary elements of preparing to lector are **training, study,** and **practice**. There are also last minute details. Training is the long-term preparation you do to get ready for your ministry. Study is more specific to the particular reading you are preparing to proclaim. Practice is what you should be doing the entire week before you are scheduled to lector.

Training

Training is long-term preparation. You may have received some training in your parish when you began your ministry. You may have received regular or periodic training in your parish after that. In any case, it is always helpful to practice proclamation in front of others who can give you constructive criticism. Training can come from a group of lectors working together or from a liturgist working with one or more lectors. Ideally, whoever trains the lectors in your parish will schedule lector formation as a regular event in your parish, at least once a year.

Your diocese may organize workshops or seminars that focus on lectoring. You might have a chance to participate in larger events, perhaps at regional or national conferences, that can help you in this ministry. Ideally, someone in your parish, perhaps the liturgist, will let you know when such events become available. Not only can you receive helpful hints on techniques at these events, you can also learn more background about Scripture in general and about the way the lectionary readings relate to each other. You can also read books such as this, which explain the "whys" and "hows" of this ministry.

Study

Part of your task as lector is to interpret the readings. How you use your voice will cause the meaning of a reading to be brought out in a specific way. Sometimes it is difficult to understand the meaning, especially in some of the Old Testament readings. Reading the verses in Scripture that precede and follow a reading make the context clearer to you. It is also useful to read commentaries. This gives you the benefit of learning from experts. This practice has made a significant difference in my own understanding of particular readings. You may find commentaries available in your parish library or even in the sacristy. If not, you might suggest that whoever is responsible for liturgy in your parish make one available. You don't need one of the very large, expensive commentaries. There are smaller books commenting on each book of the Bible. Some parishes bring the lectors together to reflect as a group on the Sunday's readings. This helps lectors develop a common perspective on the readings at their particular liturgies and allows all to benefit from the study or research done by any of them. It deepens the understanding each lector brings to his or her proclamation.

When studying the readings, it is important to understand them in various contexts: what people have heard the week or weeks before, what they will hear in the following weeks, and in relationship to the other readings for this week. Be sure to look at the psalm as well. I have heard the psalm response described as "the aura" within which the rest of the readings are understood. This may also help you understand what needs to be emphasized.

Not all the readings will be proclaimed in the same way, in the same tone of voice, or at the same volume. The readings contain stories, prophecy, poetry, laws, letters, proverbs, parables, and visions. Depending on the mood and meaning, the readings will need to be proclaimed in different ways. More than the words need to be communicated in the proclamation. Edward Foley is clear about that:

> For whether it be Law or prophets,
>> wisdom or history,
>> Gospel or epistle,
>> I am convinced that every word we enunciate and receive
>> is first and foremost a *love chronicle*:
>> an inscription about divine passion for human creatures,
>> whether that perdures on tablets, parchment,
>> scrolls, or Gospel Books.
>> Whatever its physical form or literary genre,
>> this divine utterance we honor as privileged revelation
>> is, at its core, one elongated exposé
>> of God's incomprehensible passion for humanity.
> What tradition has separated into individual biblical books, is in fact,
>> a single extended narrative—
>> refracted through multiple genres,
>> parsed into chapter and verse,
>> and edited for public proclamation.[4]

As Father Foley describes it, there are many different types of writings within the Scriptures, each with its own style of proclamation but all needing to express the divine passion for the people of God.

A lector's workbook is a great tool, especially if you don't have lectionaries at home. The lector's workbook lays out the reading as we will see it in the lectionary. It gives some background, context, and pronunciation hints. It gives proclamation suggestions, italicizing words that are "supposed" to be emphasized. I put this in quotation marks because the workbook's emphasis is only a suggestion. You need to decide for yourself if the suggested emphasis is the best one for your community on this day. Liturgy Training Publications puts out an annual workbook. There may be others available also.

One indispensable item is a pronunciation guide. If you use a lector's workbook, there may be a pronunciation guide included. If not, you might get one for yourself—they are inexpensive. It is also good to have one available in the sacristy. That way, if any last minute questions come up about pronunciation, you'll find this reference readily at hand.

This is an essential part of your preparation. You must make sure that you know how to pronounce not only the names and other difficult words peculiar to Scripture but also words from our normal vocabulary that you might stumble over. Mispronunciations are distracting. At best, they take your listeners out of the receptive mode and put them into an analytical, critical mode. They may ruin the reading. I had always thought it was an urban legend that a lector somewhere mispronounced "brazier" as "brassiere." One Sunday, I heard our own lector refer to the dreaded "smoking brassiere." In the sacristy after Mass, the priest remarked that there must have been "women's lib" back in those days, too. He tried to make light of it, but the point of the reading had been lost. The lectors who make this gaffe obviously missed part of their preparation.

Practice

Practice is what will enable you to change a reading to a proclamation. What is a "proclamation"? How is it different from "reading"? One important difference between reading and proclamation is that the proclamation is *your* faith witness, just as the Scriptures are the faith witness of the people of the time. Proclamation implies that you have delved deeply into the meaning of the reading, prayed with it, and gained insight as to its meaning both for yourself and for the community that you serve. What does God wish to convey to this community at this time? To learn this, you must make an effort to understand the community as well as the Scripture itself.

Familiarity with the specific reading will enable this faith witness in your proclamation. It will make it easier for you to make the meaning clear to your audience. It will help *you* make the reading sound as though it is being spoken specifically to them. It will help *them* hear it that way. It will draw the listeners into Scriptures.

In order to do this, you must become immersed in the reading. You must understand the characters and their motivation; you must know the story and its context; and you must be able to express this through tone, inflection, tempo, volume, and style. These are things to consider when you practice. However, you must practice enough so that these things become an integral part of your relationship to the reading. Then, when you proclaim the reading, you will communicate unselfconsciously.

If a different lector is used for each reading (the preferred arrangement), take some time to practice the reading assigned to the other lector. If the other lector can't make it for some reason and you are called upon at the last minute to do both readings, you will be prepared.

Last-Minute Details

On the day you are to lector, a few details need your attention. For example, you will want to begin the day early enough so that you do not feel harried and can be relaxed. Plan ahead to dress in a manner appropriate for this ministry. Sometimes people say, "God doesn't care how I dress." I would say, "That is true, but … ." When we are ministering, we dress not just for ourselves, but for the whole community. We are God's representatives in what we do, and we dress to show God's respect—and ours—for members of the community. Catholic liturgy is one in which the participants are washed with the water of baptism, fed in the Eucharist, and anointed with oil at baptism, confirmation, holy orders, and the anointing of the sick. At special Masses, they are incensed as a mark of their dignity. In the context of the liturgy, we show respect for one another as members of the Body of Christ, for Christ present in each of us. We also show respect for the God whom we serve through our ministry and for the ministry we are privileged to exercise.

You will also want to arrive at the church early enough to make sure everything is in order. You don't want to feel rushed. Be sure that the lectionary is where you expect it to be. If *The Book of the*

Preparation

Gospels is to be processed up, be sure that you, or whoever is to process it up, has it in hand. Otherwise, be sure it is where it will be needed during the liturgy. Don't take for granted that someone will have done that for you.

Be sure that the lectionary is set up (marked with the ribbon) correctly. You don't want to hunt for your place. To be safe, memorize the page number so that you can easily find your reading if the ribbon somehow falls out of place. Because the three cycles are in one book, it can be difficult to locate the correct readings, especially if you're under pressure in front of the assembly.

If you will be using a microphone, check it. Verify that it is on and that it is in the correct position for the person who will use it first. The microphone should be aimed at your chin. You should need to project in order for the microphone to amplify your voice, and it should not obscure your face.

If you are reading the intercessions or the announcements, be sure you know where they are and that they are in place for the liturgy. Arrive early enough to practice them. The intercessions may have names in them that are difficult to pronounce. Try asking the priest—who may know the person—how to pronounce the name. Or ask someone else who speaks the language from which this name comes or who may otherwise be able to assist you. If you can't find anyone who knows for sure how to pronounce the name, work on it to make it sound as smooth as possible. When it's time to say the name, pronounce it however you have decided with no hesitation or stumbling. Say it with assurance so that the community is not distracted from their prayer by the mechanics of your pronunciation.

This is a very good general rule for liturgy: Don't let the mechanics show. Make your efforts as seamless as possible so that people can flow with the liturgy in their hearts and not be brought up into their heads. Move slowly and respectfully, remain calm and self-assured, speak slowly and distinctly, and have everything in place for smooth transitions.

Be sure that the other lector has arrived (if two are scheduled). Otherwise, you may need to proclaim both readings.

All this attention to detail requires arriving early. You need time to check everything and make sure it's in its place. You need to practice what needs to be practiced. When all of this is complete, you need to greet the incoming parishioners. Many parishes also have the practice of gathering all the ministers for a brief prayer, either in the sacristy before going out to greet people or out in the vestibule itself. The prayer can be led by the presider, by the liturgist, or by any one of the ministers. It is a brief chance to focus on what we are about and to put ourselves in God's hands, asking for God's guidance in our ministry.

After Mass

After the dismissal, as a courtesy to those coming to minister for the next Sunday or weekday Mass, be sure everything is where it can be found easily when needed. *The Book of the Gospels* is not processed out at the end of Mass, but sometimes it will have been processed out for the dismissal of the catechumens. In either case, it will need to be retrieved and put back in its place for the next Mass.

Chapter Six
Specific Techniques

Eugene A. Walsh, S.S., a Vatican II liturgist, was enthused about the role of the assembly and about the ministry of the laity. He was excited about the elevation of the Liturgy of the Word to equal importance with the Liturgy of the Eucharist. In this abbreviated excerpt from one of his writings, he imagines Jesus speaking to us every Sunday.

> "My people! My people! Do you hear me? Are you listening? Really listening? It is Sunday morning, the ten o'clock mass. This is Jesus speaking with you. I am trying to get your attention. I want you to listen. I have much to say to you, and so little time. Will you listen? ...
>
> "I want to tell you how much my Father loves you. I want to tell you how much I love you. ...
>
> "I want to tell you my story all over again. I want to tell you my story because it is not just my story. My story is every bit as much your story. I want us to share our story together. It is the story of our living and our dying together and of our rising together to a wonderful and exciting new life. It is the story of our journey together from prison to freedom. It is the story of our freedom march. ...

"Help me to become a living and life-giving voice all over again in the midst of our world today. I need your voices to become a life-giving word at your Sunday mass. I need your voices to be heard. I have no other voice. ... If you tell the story well, I will live again in your midst. ...

"So please speak up. Proclaim our story. Shout it out. Taste it. Feel it. Get it into your own flesh and bones. Tell it with such strength and faith and feeling that the people of this assembly will not be able to stop listening. Get their attention and hold it. Don't let them go. ...

"You see, I am really present with you here when you proclaim my word on Sunday in the midst of your assembly. I am actually here speaking with you in the very moment that you hear my word. ... My word at this moment is for you and for no one else. I never spoke this exact word to you before, and never will again."[5]

With this in mind, let us proceed to discuss how we can make this word live in our assemblies.

Practice Techniques

One way to begin practice for a specific reading is to work with a partner. This can be another lector, a friend, a prayer partner, or a family member. Ask this person to listen to your reading and then tell you what primary thoughts or images came up as you were reading. Next, have your partner read the passage while you listen and notice what thoughts or images seem primary to you. This technique will give you a preliminary feeling for the reading. You can do this a couple of times. It is amazing how human beings hear different things each time they hear the

Specific Techniques 25

reading. This will catechize you and give you new insight and understanding.

Some parishes gather all the lectors for the coming weekend for a communal practice session. In this setting, all can share their insights and what they might have learned about the reading from commentaries or other sources, pray over the readings, and practice them together.

Become intimately familiar with the reading. This does not mean you should memorize it. It is, after all, a reading. However, you should be able to tell someone in your own words what the reading is about and how the content unfolds in the course of the excerpt. This will help free you from the need to look at the book constantly while you are reading.

Practice by reading out loud. You may want to record yourself and play it back to see what you might want to improve. Are you speaking slowly enough? Are there enough pauses? Are you enunciating clearly? If your recording is a video, it is even better. You can see your posture, your eye contact, your composure, and so forth. The words you will speak are important to the life of the community. You must make sure that all can hear and understand.

Practice by reading out loud. Read each sentence a number of different ways, placing the emphasis on a different word each time. Even if you have a lector's workbook, you may find that a different emphasis works best for you. See which one makes the most sense to you, which way of emphasizing it seems to communicate the meaning most clearly.

Emphasis

Practice by reading out loud. Besides emphasizing specific words within each sentence, you want to identify the part of each reading that is the most important. It may not be the same sentence every time you read it. Determine which sentence seems most important on this occasion, then emphasize it. Emphasizing a word generally requires you to put more stress on that word. In order to emphasize a thought or sentence, read it more slowly than the rest of the reading. This will also help you to highlight the sentence and still emphasize a particular word within that sentence. In addition, you can set a sentence off from the rest of the reading with a pause before you begin the sentence and following it. This will cue your listeners to be particularly attentive because something important is coming and has just been said.

Sample from the first reading for the First Sunday of Advent (C): Jer 33:16

> In those days Judah shall be safe
> and Jerusalem shall dwell secure;
>
> *Pause briefly.*
> this is what they shall call her:
>
> *Pause. Then read more slowly, the last three words very deliberately.*
> "The LORD our justice."
>
> *Pause. Then read with authority.*
> The word of the Lord.

Tempo

Practice by reading out loud. In the course of the reading, you may use different tempos, especially if it is a narrative story. You can set off the actual narrative from the parts spoken by the characters by giving them a different cadence and tempo to communicate the feelings of the character. This will help the story come alive for your listeners. It will make it more interesting and communicate the varying importance of the different parts of the reading.

Sample from the first reading for the Seventh Sunday of Easter (B): Acts 1:15-16

>*Proclaim with authority.*
>A reading from the Acts of the Apostles
>
>*Pause.*
>*State matter-of-factly.*
>Peter stood up in the midst of the brothers
>
>*Read more quickly. This is an explanation.*
>—there was a group of about one hundred and twenty
>   persons
>in the one place—.
>
>*State matter-of-factly.*
>He said,
>
>*More emphatically.*
>"My brothers,
>   the Scripture had to be fulfilled

A little more quickly.
> which the Holy Spirit spoke beforehand
> through the mouth of David, concerning Judas,
> who was the guide for those who arrested Jesus."

Eye Contact

One way I describe the difference between reading and proclaiming is to say that it is the difference between *reading a story* and *telling a story*. Imagine that you are with your child or grandchild. How will your presentation differ between reading a story and telling a story? We describe saying something from memory as saying it "by heart." Even though I am not suggesting that you memorize the reading, I am suggesting that you proclaim it from the heart in order to speak to the hearts of your listeners.

One way to convey that you are telling the story instead of reading it is to use eye contact. This form of physical communication is what you use when you tell a story to a child or to another adult. It helps make the story real and immediate for them.

Now let's talk about how you will apply this technique when you proclaim your reading for the assembly.

When you come up to the ambo, verify that the lectionary is open to your reading. When you are ready, look at the assembly. Let your gaze move from one side to the other, including everyone and encouraging them to look at you. If people are coming in late, wait for them to be seated. In this way, you make sure the assembly is ready to hear your reading. This is an act of hospitality.

Many parishes do not use missalettes because they want members of the assembly to look at and listen to the lector instead of reading from the missalette. Although it is advisable to have some missalettes available for those who have difficulty hearing, it is preferable for there to be a visual connection between members of the assembly and the lector. You will have a hard time making eye contact if all the heads are focused on the booklet. Dan F. Onley, in an article designed as an insert in parish bulletins, wrote on the use of missalettes:

> As for listening to God's word proclaimed aloud, it is difficult to imagine exactly how the reading of a book can be done at the same time we are listening to a person speaking aloud the living word of God.[6]

Even if your parish uses missalettes, your best chance of getting eye contact is right at the beginning. Wait. People will look up to see why the reading hasn't started. Now say, "A reading from ..." while looking at them. Now they know you're speaking to *them*. Having established eye contact, they are much less likely to go back to their missalettes.

Then look down to the reading that you now know so well, get the first sense line in your mind, and look up to proclaim it. (By a "sense line" I mean a sentence or part of a sentence that you will proclaim as a unit. The length of a particular sense line depends on what it takes to make the meaning clear.) My rule of thumb is that when your mouth is open, you should be looking up. When you look down, you should not be speaking. This can be pretty scary. It takes practice. I encourage using a finger to mark your place, which will make it easy to find the next sense line when you look down. Then you can look up again to proclaim that one. This is one reason it is helpful to practice in front of a mirror. You can watch yourself and be sure that you are making eye contact while you are saying the words.

Speak slowly and distinctly. This is especially important in a large or resonant building. Depending on the text, you can read some parts faster than others.

Sample from the first reading on the Sixteenth Sunday in Ordinary Time (C): Gn 18:1-10a

> *In a storytelling voice, connect the first three lines.*
> The LORD appeared to **Abraham** by the terebinth of Mamre,
> > as he sat in the entrance of his tent,
> > while the day was growing hot.
>
> *Pause for a deep breath. Then speak more slowly.*
> Looking up, Abraham saw three men standing nearby.
>
> *Increase tempo slightly to indicate excitement.*
> When he saw them, he ran from the entrance of the tent to greet them;
>
> *Say slightly more emphatically.*
> > and bowing to the ground, he said:
>
> *In a conversational voice, speak as if trying convince someone.*
> > "Sir, if I may ask you this favor,
> > please do not go on past your servant.
> > Let some water be brought, that you may bathe your feet,
> > and then rest yourselves under the tree.
> > Now that you have come this close to your servant,
> > let me bring you a little food, that you may refresh yourselves;
> > and afterwards you may go on your way."

Breathe deeply, begin in storytelling tone, and then speak as the men would speak.
The men replied, "Very well, do as you have said."

Increase tempo to indicate Abraham's haste.
Abraham hastened into the tent and told Sarah,

With emphasis, engage Sarah's help.
"Quick, three measures of fine flour! Knead it and make rolls."

Continue at the faster tempo.
He ran to the herd, picked out a tender, choice steer,
and gave it to a servant, who quickly prepared it.

A little more slowly and deliberately.
Then Abraham got some curds and milk,
as well as the steer that had been prepared,
and set these before the three men;
and he waited on them under the tree while they ate.

Pause briefly, use your storytelling voice, and then your questioning voice.
They asked Abraham, "Where is your wife Sarah?"

Again, use your storytelling voice, and then reply as Abraham would.
He replied, "There in the tent."

Use your storytelling voice. Then speak slowly and deliberately.
One of them said, "I will surely return to you about this
time next year,

Speak slowly and emphatically (this is great news).
and Sarah will then have a son."

Pause. Then declare emphatically.
The word of the Lord.

I have not put the emphases in except for the first line. This was to make sure that Abraham connected to "he" in the next line. Experiment with where you put the emphasis on the words to make the story engaging. With this text, you really are telling a story.

Another advantage of speaking more slowly is that it gives you time to look down between sense lines without breaking the flow. It's just a natural function of reading. Many times when reading, lectors (or presiders) use what I call the "head-bobbing" technique. Their heads bob up and down in an attempt to glance at the assembly, but they never look up long enough to be convincing. This can be rather dizzying to watch.

Conviction

Remember that you are speaking God's word to the people in front of you. Let them know that you are speaking to them. This is not a performance. This is a heart-to-heart faith witness of the word that you have studied and prayed. Your conviction should be obvious, and it should convince your listeners that you believe what you are saying, you believe that it is important, and you believe that it is important for them to hear and understand. You should convey a sense of urgency.

Energy

Communicating your conviction requires energy. Many times lectors stand close to the microphone, speak quietly, and expect that the microphone will amplify them. Which it will. However, what it amplifies is a quiet little voice without energy. You need *energy* to carry your conviction, stir the hearts of your listeners, and let them know that what you say is important for *them*. Don't depend on the microphone. Project your voice to the person in the last pew. Let your eagerness to have them hear you be obvious. If this voice is too loud for the microphone, back away from it. Let God's word ring throughout the building. Even without the microphone, you should be able to hear your own voice bouncing off the back wall—not in a deafening way but enough to let you know it's reaching all the way to the back. People shouldn't have to strain to hear you. Energy is one of your most important tools.

Inflection

When you are working on making the readings intelligible to the community, your use of inflection will make a big difference. We all look for those audible clues to meaning in everyday speech. When the tone goes up at the end of a sentence, we understand it as a question. When the tone drops, we know we're at the end of a sentence.

Sample from the first reading on the Third Sunday of Advent (A): Is 35:1-6a, 10

> *Read with expectant excitement.*
> The desert and the parched land will exult;
>   the steppe will rejoice and bloom.
> They will bloom with abundant flowers,
>   and rejoice with joyful song.
> The glory of Lebanon will be given to them,
>   the splendor of Carmel and Sharon;
> they will see the glory of the LORD,
>   the splendor of our God.

Pause briefly. Then continue just a little more slowly, giving directions.

Strengthen the hands that are feeble,
> Make firm the knees that are weak,
say to those whose hearts are frightened:

Speak with a stronger, deeper voice—and more slowly.
> Be strong, fear not!

Even more slowly and emphatically.
Here is your God,
> He comes with vindication;
Keep voice up to suggest that more to this sentence is coming (or you could choose to make it a new sentence).
with divine recompense
> he comes to save you.

Pause briefly. Then speak more quickly but emphatically.
Then will the eyes of the blind be opened,
> The ears of the deaf be cleared;
then will the lame leap like a stag,
> then the tongue of the mute will sing.

Pause very briefly. Then speak slowly and with more emphasis.
Those whom the LORD has ransomed will return
> and enter Zion singing,
Keep voice up, more is coming.
> crowned with everlasting joy;

More slowly, more emphasis.
they will meet with **joy** and **gladness,**

Specific Techniques 35

> *Pause briefly. Then speak more slowly, emphasizing the first, third, and fifth word. Your inflection drops at the end.*
> **sorrow** and **mourning** will **flee.**
>
> *Pause. Then say with conviction.*
> The **word** of the **Lord.**

Even within a sentence, inflection can be important.

Sample from the first reading for the Ascension of the Lord (A): Acts 1:1

> In the first book, Theophilus,
> I dealt with all that Jesus did and taught ...

Very often, when this sentence is read, it sounds like "Theophilus" is the name of that first book. It should be read so that people understand that Theophilus is the name of the person who is being addressed. Emphasize "first" to make it clear you are addressing Theophilus. Try it both ways and see what the difference is.

For some readings, especially some of St. Paul's "epistles of the run-on sentence," it is a challenge to make the meaning apparent. The only technique that works is signaling with your tone that the sentence has not yet come to an end. Sometimes, a reading from one of St. Paul's letters will be most of a page long but only two or three sentences. For a long sentence, you can't let your voice drop or people will think that it's the end of the sentence. Then they will believe your next words will begin a new sentence. Because they don't begin a sentence, the words will be incomplete and won't make sense. Your listeners won't know what to connect them to. It takes thought and practice to bring out the full meaning of one of St. Paul's very long sentences.

Sample from the second reading on the Fifth Sunday in Ordinary Time (A): I Cor 2:1-5

> When I came to you, brothers and sisters,
> proclaiming the mystery of God,

Keep voice tone up, more is coming.

> I did not come with sublimity of words or of wisdom.
> For I resolved to know nothing while I was with you

Connect to this next phrase without pause as though they were written in one line, but emphasize "Jesus Christ."

> except Jesus Christ,

Pause very briefly. Then emphasize "him" to connect it back to "Jesus Christ."

> and him crucified.

Pause briefly before continuing.
I came to you in weakness and fear and much trembling,
Keep voice up, more is coming.

> And my message and my proclamation
> were not with persuasive words of wisdom,

Read these two lines as one. Keep tone up, more is coming.

> but with a demonstration of Spirit and power,

Keep voice up. Continue as if one line.

> so that your faith might rest not on human wisdom

Keep voice up. Then slow down and emphasize …

> but on the **power** of **God**.

Pause. Then declare definitively …

The **word** of the **Lord**.

Specific Techniques 37

Experiment with it. You can use different tones, depending on the text, to suggest there is more to come. It is impossible to demonstrate this on a written page, so you will need to play with it in order to find out what works best.

For example, sometimes you can emphasize a word that is an antecedent of what is to follow in the next lines. This will help people hear the references more clearly.

Sample from the second reading on the Fifteenth Sunday in Ordinary Time (C): Col 1:15-18

> *Emphasize the first two words because on them hang the rest of the reading.*
> **Christ Jesus** is the image of the invisible God,
>   the firstborn of all creation.
>
> *Now emphasize "him" to connect back to "Christ Jesus."*
> For in **him** were created **all** things in heaven and on earth,
>   the visible and the invisible,
>   whether thrones or dominions or principalities or powers;
>
> *In this next line, you can also emphasize the prepositions "through" and "for."*
>   all things were created **through him** and **for him**.
>
> *Emphasize "He" to connect to "Christ Jesus" and emphasize this entire phrase.*
> **He** is before all things,
>
> *Emphasize "him" and "all" with a very slight pause between.*
>   and in **him all** things hold together.

Emphasize "He" in the next three lines, plus other words to make the meaning clear.
He is the head of the **body**, the **church**.
He is the **beginning**, the **firstborn** from the dead,
    that in all things **he himself** might be preeminent.

This is one suggestion. Play with it. It may be that emphasizing different or additional words will help you bring out the meaning. The main point here is to look at how to use emphasis on words so that they will be in people's minds as you continue the reading and help them to connect to the references just proclaimed or to come.

Sometimes you can break a long sentence in two, but you will have to read each part so that it makes sense as a separate sentence. You have to work this out in practice. What will make the most sense? This is another situation where it's helpful to practice with someone else who can give you feedback.

Sample from the second reading on Christmas (Day): Heb 1:1-2

  Brothers and sisters:
  In times past, God spoke in partial and various ways
      to our ancestors through the prophets;

  You can treat this semicolon as a period and start the following as a new sentence.

    in these last days, he has spoken to us through the Son,
      whom he made heir of all things ...

Movement

How you move is important. When it's time to go up for the reading, stand up and let your posture carry conviction and authority. While this is not a time to show personal pride, it is a time to express the importance of your ministry. This should be obvious in the way you carry yourself as you go to the ambo. Moving quickly is distracting and communicates undesirable messages, perhaps insecurity or self-consciousness. Your carriage should demonstrate confidence. What you are about to do is important. You will speak God's word to God's people. Your walk and stance should reflect this.

Whether you bow to the altar on the way to the ambo depends on your path to the ambo (whether you are crossing in front of the altar) and the tradition of your parish. It is traditional in some parishes and not in others. One issue is how it looks to those seated behind the person bowing to the altar.

Silence

Once you get to the ambo, make sure your microphone is adjusted properly for you, be sure the lectionary is open to the correct page, bring to mind the first statement you are going to make, and look out over the assembly to engage their attention. Your silence at this time will be palpable. It will encourage all to look up. Even if they have been "zoned out," the cessation of words will catch their attention. If people are being seated at this time, give them time to complete that action before you begin. You do not want any distractions. Then, when you have their attention, look at them and make that first statement declaring the source of the reading.

Another type of silence is the pause during the reading that sets off the more important messages of the reading. This is a briefer period of silence. Once in a while, because of the nature of the narrative, it helps to put a very brief pause between sections to set up a change of scene or mood. This might be just a deeper, slower breath.

At the end of the reading, you should pause briefly before saying, "The word of the Lord." This also calls attention to the importance of what you are going to say. These words should be proclaimed with the same energy as the rest of the reading. It should carry sufficient conviction to invite the people's response. "Thanks be to God."

At this time, the liturgy calls for a time of silence to reflect on the word that has been heard. This brief period of reflective silence occurs in most parishes between the time the lector has returned to his or her seat in the assembly and the moment the cantor gets up to introduce the responsorial psalm or the gospel alleluia. There is a problem with this. My observation is that as soon as the lector moves away from the ambo, the people are finished with the reading and are ready to move on to the next part of the liturgy. The moment of reflective silence doesn't work because people are wondering why the musicians are taking so long for their next part.

I would like to suggest the following technique, which has worked well in my parish.

After the people have voiced their "Thanks be to God," don't move except to bow your head. Don't move away from the ambo. Don't turn the page. Don't move the ribbon. Model the reflectiveness into which the people are invited at this time. How long should this period of silence be? One of our lectors suggested as long as it takes to slowly say the "Glory Be." This seems to work. When the time seems right, move the ribbon, close the book, or do whatever is necessary to prepare for the next part, and return to your seat. If you don't move, you won't pull people out of their

Specific Techniques

reflective mode and start them thinking about the next part of the liturgy. This technique will work after the first or second readings.

Focus

A similar disruption in flow can occur around the general intercessions or prayer of the faithful. In some parishes, the lector goes to the ambo during the reciting of the Creed in order to be ready for these intercessions. When this happens, the lector does not participate with the community in affirming the common statement of belief. This suggests the lector has more important things to do. Moreover, the movement of the lector is distracting to the assembly, which is supposed to be reciting the Creed. It sends the message that efficiency is more important than prayerfulness.

You need to follow the custom of your parish, but it is better in my view to proceed to the ambo as soon as the Creed is finished. If there are other rites that will change the flow of the liturgy at this time, you need to find out about these in advance so you know when to move up to the ambo.

When you get to the ambo to do the intercessions, open the binder containing the intercessions. Then look at the presider, who introduces them with an invitation to prayer. If you look at him, everyone else will look in his direction, too. The focus belongs on him.

After the presider's invitation to prayer, announce each intention followed by a brief pause before saying, "We pray to the Lord," or whatever wording is used. Your pause gives the people the opportunity to make the intention their own and to add their individual intentions to it. After your invitation, they can say,

"Lord, hear our prayer," or whatever response is used in your parish.

When you finish announcing the intentions, don't go back to your seat or even close the binder. That may be tempting, but such movement will distract from the concluding prayer, which the presider says. Instead, when you finish your part, turn to face the presider and look at him as he does his concluding prayer. This will draw the community's focus to him and facilitate their participation in the prayer. When he is finished, close the binder, place it wherever it's supposed to go, and return to your seat.

The announcements, usually at the end of Mass following the post-communion prayer, are a little different. In this case, after the presider has concluded the prayer, walk to the microphone that is used for the announcements and read them. The announcements are an integral part of the liturgy. They help the transition between the liturgy celebrated within the church walls and the ministry we are called to during the week. Many times what is read in the announcements is what we are being dismissed to do at the end of Mass. "Go in peace to love and serve the Lord and one another."

You may want to remain at the microphone for the final blessing and dismissal. If you are part of the procession of ministers, you can process out from there. If you are not, you can return to your seat and process out with the rest of the assembly.

After Mass

Before you leave, there are a few housekeeping points to remember. Be sure the lectionary is returned to the sacristy or wherever the next lector will expect to find it. If it is the last Mass of the day, return it to wherever it is kept during the week. If you are responsible for setting up the microphone, you may need to put that away as well at the end of the day. Any binders or other books used during the liturgy need to be returned to the location where they can be found by whoever needs them next.

Chapter Seven
Preparing to Lector—A Checklist

Advance Preparation—Begin at least a week ahead.

- ☐ Know what reading you have been assigned.

- ☐ Read the parts before and after it in the Bible.
  This will help to set the context for the reading and help you to understand the reading.

- ☐ Read what comes the week(s) before and after in the lectionary.
  Although all the readings in the lectionary are from the Bible, the lectionary is not the Bible. The readings, in addition to their biblical context, relate to each other in a liturgical context. They relate to the other readings within the day—and to readings of the week(s) before and the week(s) after. Studying these relationships will help you understand the context in which the people will hear and understand a particular reading.

- ☐ Start reading aloud, if possible to someone else.
  Ask them what struck them about the reading. This will help you hear what you are emphasizing.

Preparing to Lector—A Checklist

- ❏ **Be sure you know the correct pronunciation of words.** Watch out for words you don't use every day (like "brazier"); words that can be confusing like "prophecy" (the noun) and "prophesy" (the verb); proper names like "Golgatha" and "Arimathea." The lector's workbooks should have pronunciations. Or you can purchase a pronunciation guide.

- ❏ **Experiment with different emphases to see what makes the word come alive for you.**
  Different emphases convey different meanings. See which one seems to fit best.

- ❏ **If you use a lector's workbook, look at their background information and suggestions.**
  Remember, they are just suggestions. The workbook's idea of where to put the emphasis in a sentence may not be what works for you and your community at this time.

- ❏ **Have your own community in mind as you prepare.**
  Prepare to speak God's word to your specific community. The reading should be directed to the listeners.

- ❏ **Be sure you are familiar with the routine of your parish.**
  Know which lector does what during the liturgy. Know where to find the books or other items you may need. Be sure you know whatever is necessary to know about the microphone.

- ❏ **PRACTICE!**
  Practice should make a reading so familiar to you that it will be a faith sharing with your community. The passage should become so familiar that you do not read it so much

as tell a well-known story. Practice all the nuances of how you might read a passage. This will help change it from a reading to a proclamation.

Things to work on when you are practicing

- ❑ **Energy!**
  This is a necessity for good proclamation. The energy you project will help the reading assume importance. The listeners will know it is important to you, and they will be drawn to listen to your conviction.

- ❑ **Practice as though there will be no microphone.**
  Speak to the back of the building. If you speak into the microphone and depend on it to carry your voice, you will lack the necessary energy. The energy with which you speak communicates enthusiasm and urgency.

- ❑ **Practice looking up while you are speaking.**
  Avoid "head bobbing." Know the story well enough so that you can look up while you are saying the words and look down only during the pauses for breath. This is a story you are telling. It should feel like you are communicating directly to the members of the assembly, not just reading to them.

- ❑ **Decide what the most important line of the reading is for this day.**
  Set it off from the rest of the reading with pauses, and read it more slowly and deliberately.

- ❑ **Practice using pauses where appropriate so people have time to absorb what you are reading.**
  Take time for an extra deep breath when there is some change in the reading. It will set your listeners up to hear it.

- ❏ **Change your vocal expression to suit the mood and setting of the text.**
  Depending on what you are reading, you may need several styles of proclamation.

- ❏ **Change your tempo.**
  The most important part should be read the most slowly to give it emphasis and time to sink in. Suit your tempo and expression to the meaning and style of the reading.

- ❏ **Take particular care with your inflection at the end of a line.**
  When you reach the end of a sentence, let your voice drop. This cues your listeners to expect a new sentence. If you need to pause but the sentence will continue, keep the tone of your voice up. This cues your listeners that there is more to come. If you drop your voice, you make the section sound like the end of a sentence, in which case people will assume that the next part is a new sentence. They will be left in confusion when it turns out to be an incomplete statement.

Proximate preparation—the day of the liturgy

- ❏ Give yourself time to get ready so that you are not rushed. Arrive early.

- ❏ Dress appropriately, in a way that is respectful of the community and of your ministry.

- ❏ Locate the lectionary. In case the ribbon gets moved, memorize the page number for your reading.

- ❏ Locate the binder(s) or other book(s) containing the intercessions and announcements.

- ❏ Verify pronunciation of names in the intercessions.
- ❏ Practice the intercessions.
- ❏ Practice the announcements.
- ❏ Be sure the microphone is set up, turned on, and adjusted for your height.
- ❏ Check the volume of the microphone, and adjust it if necessary.
- ❏ Be sure there is sufficient lighting.
- ❏ Ask if there is a special rite at this Mass that might change the flow of the liturgy and affect the timing of your parts of the liturgy.
- ❏ Gather for prayer with the other ministers.
- ❏ Go out front to greet other parishioners as they arrive.
- ❏ In the procession, walk with grace and poise, confident in your ministry.
- ❏ Carry the lectionary high and with reverence. Let it be a presence.

When it's time to read ...

- ❏ Approach the ambo purposefully, slowly, with grace and authority.

It is God's word you will be reading. The proclamation begins when you leave your seat and ends when you return to your seat.

Preparing to Lector—A Checklist

- ❑ **Establish eye contact.**
  Wait until people are seated, the shuffling has settled down, and you have your listeners' attention.

- ❑ **Keep your finger on the text.**
  This way, you can look up to proclaim the words but find your place easily when you look down to remind yourself of the next "sense line."

- ❑ **Looking at the members of the assembly, proclaim authoritatively, "A reading from …"**
  When you look at the assembly, include the entire assembly.

- ❑ **Look at all parts of the seating area.**

- ❑ **Don't rush.**
  Keep the tempo you have practiced.

- ❑ **Enunciate clearly.**

- ❑ **Speak to the listeners in the back of the building.**

- ❑ **Use energy to project excitement and enthusiasm.**
  This is God's word, which God, through you, is speaking to them this day.

- ❑ **Remember to vary inflection and tempo as you read.**
  Actually, you should have practiced so much that you don't have to "remember." Your inflection and tempo should be natural as you adjust to the sense and style of the reading.

- ❑ **Pause slightly at the end of the reading before saying, "The word of the Lord."**

- ❑ **Read "The word of the Lord" with the same authority as the rest of the reading.**
  This is also a proclamation.

- ❑ **Don't rush.**
  There should be a period of silence for reflection after the reading. You should be in no hurry to leave the ambo and get back to your seat.

- ❑ **Consider bowing your head after saying, "The word of the Lord."**
  This will invite people into reflection on the word. After a brief period of silence, turn the page in the book, or put it aside to make room for *The Book of the Gospels*, and start to move. As soon as you start to move, you encourage the people to move on to the next thing.

- ❑ **Walk back to your pew with the same deliberate and graceful stride that you used to approach the ambo.**

- ❑ **Participate in the remainder of the liturgy (as you did before the reading) along with the rest of the assembly.**

Lector's Prayer

Heavenly Father,

Thank you for calling me to this ministry to your people.

Thank you for giving us your Word in your Son, Jesus Christ. May my reading proclaim his presence.

Send your Holy Spirit to guide me in understanding how you wish to have your word heard this day in this place. May it be alive on my tongue.

Assist me to proclaim your word clearly and with conviction.

Keep me from false pride or arrogance. Let me serve your people with humility, knowing that I, also, need to be nourished by the word I proclaim.

Help my proclamation move your people to give you thanks and praise in the Liturgy of the Eucharist in acknowledgement of the good you have done for us throughout history.

I ask you this through your Son in the power of the Holy Spirit.

Amen.

Continued Growth in Ministry

The word of God is alive. It speaks to us in many ways. It is multi-faceted and many-layered. We cannot exhaust its meaning.

Growth in the knowledge and understanding of Scripture can be achieved through books on Scripture and through Scripture study. Attending workshops can not only inform but also energize you. Meeting with other lectors on a regular basis can be helpful. Some parishes have the lectors meet each week before they read to discuss the readings and share what they have learned and understand about them. This can deepen each lector's proclamation.

Growth in the ministry of proclamation can be achieved by attending workshops given by the diocese or within your home parish. Practicing with a tape recorder or even better, a video recorder, can give insight into what improvements you can make. Practicing with other lectors, who give each other feedback and support, can help you identify and improve techniques that need improvement.

Listen to other lectors. Hear what works or doesn't work, and learn from them.

Keep practicing.

Keep reading aloud.

—Caroline Thomas

Notes

1. Rev. Edward Foley, Capuchin, *The Eucharist as Mystagogy Volume V: The Word Resounds CD* (Franklin Park, IL: World Library Publications, 2003)

2. Ibid.

3. Ibid.

4. Ibid.

5. Eugene A. Walsh, *Proclaiming God's Love in Word and Deed* (Portland, OR: OCP Publications, 1994).

6. Dan F. Onley, "Missalettes: What Do We Use Them For?" *Parish: 2000 A.D. Bulletin Supplement*, no. SP021 (Ormond Beach, FL: Pastoral Arts Associates of North America. 1984, 1992).